# Eat Pedal Sleep Repeat

## Cycling the Blue Ridge Parkway

## Jason Sullivan

Pine Grove Press

The events and conversations in this book have been set down to the best of the author's ability. This trip was taken in 2013. Names may have been changed to protect privacy.

Blue Ridge Parkway maps taken from the National Parks Service online. No protection is claimed in original U.S. Government works. Elevation map taken from BlueRidgeParkwayDaily.com. Every effort has been made to trace the copyright holders and obtain permission for the use of these images. The publisher would be grateful if notified of any corrections that should be incorporated in future reprints and editions of this book.

Photographs used with permission.

Cover photo by Hugo Andrew on Unsplash

ISBN 978-1-7341409-1-0 (paperback)

1   1   8   2   1

Thank you


Chris, whose love for Christ, nature, and others
always inspires me.

and

Jim and Susan, who took the time to look after us.



(Clipped from an email from Susan after we returned.)

...with the special love for all cyclists and their
endeavors may we say the old Irish blessing:

"May the wind be at your back, and may the
road rise up to greet you...and may God
hold you in the palm of His hand."

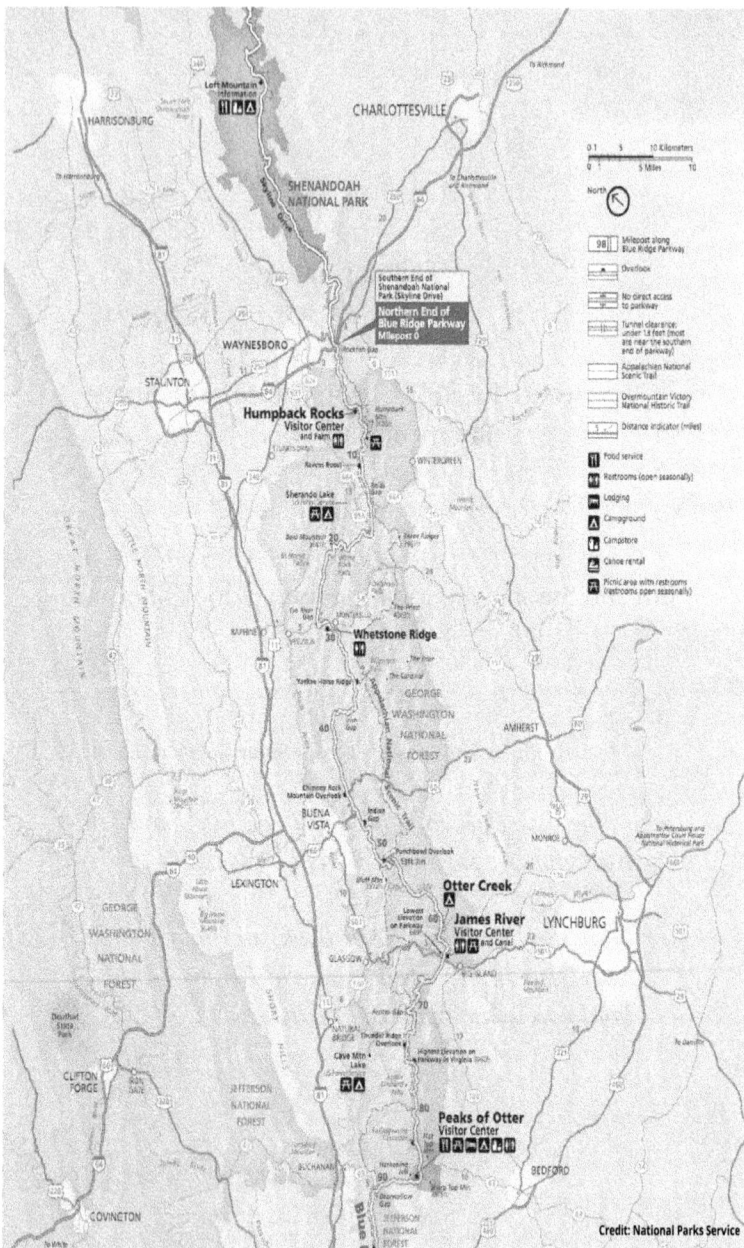

Credit: National Parks Service

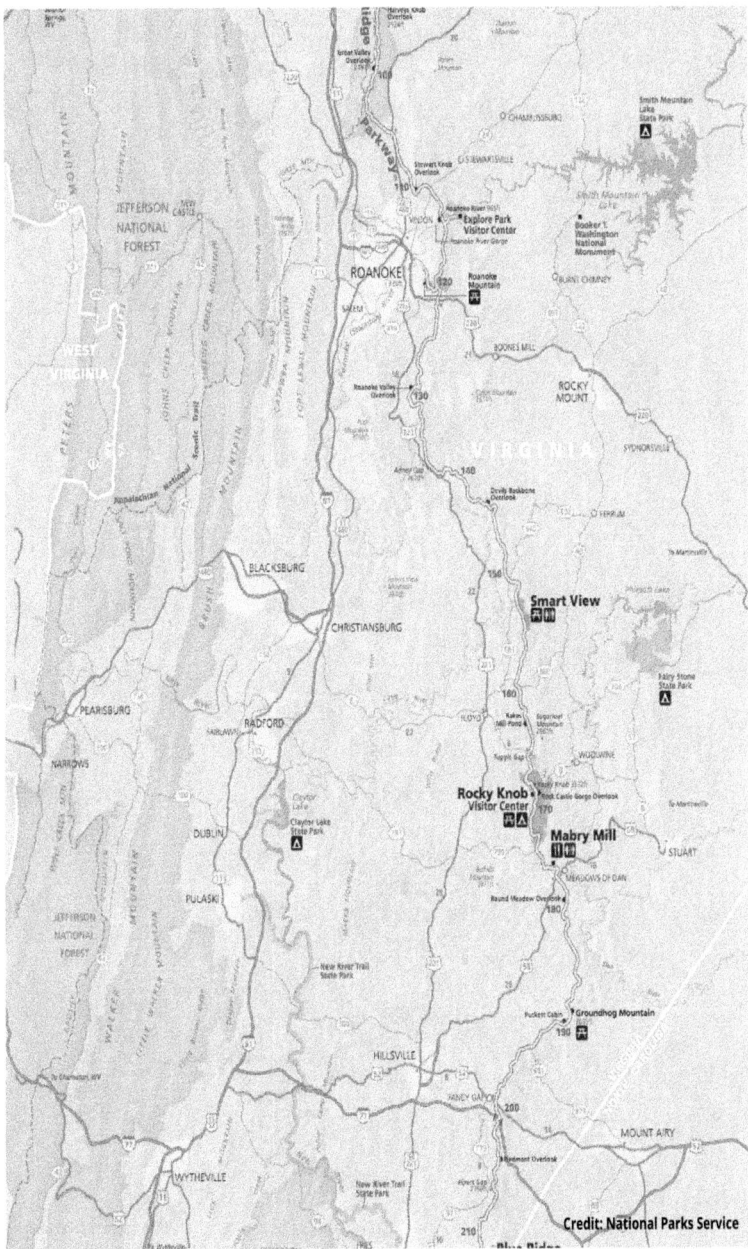

Credit: National Parks Service

NATIONAL
FOREST

GALAX

Blue Ridge
**Music Center**
Visitor Center

RURAL
RETREAT

R
I
D
G
E

**Cumberland Knob**

Fox Hunters Paradise

220

Blue Ridge Parkway

JEFFERSON
NATIONAL
FOREST

INDEPENDENCE

ROARING

MARION

SUGAR GROVE

230

Little Glade
Mill Pond

SPARTA

TWIN
OAKS

Stone Mountain
State Park

Air Bellows Gap

240

Brinegar Cabin

**Doughton
Park**
Visitor Center

To Shatin

Grayson
Highlands
State Park

New
River
State
Park

LAUREL SPRINGS

250

B
L
U
E

**Northwest Trading Post**

GLENDALE SPRINGS

260

Sheets Gap / Phillips Gap 3521

Mt Jefferson
State Natural Area

WEST
JEFFERSON

The Lump

Jumpin Gap

DAMASCUS

270

**E.B. Jeffress
Park**

Tompkins Knob Overlook
Jesse Brown Cabin

Elk
Knob
State
Park

DEEP GAP

The Cascades

MOUNTAIN
CITY

260

CHEROKEE
NATIONAL
FOREST

BOONE

Daniel Boone's Trace

South
Holston
Lake

**Moses H. Cone
Memorial Park**
Visitor Center
Craft Store

280

**BLOWING ROCK**

**Julian Price
Memorial Park**

Grandfather Inn

300

**Linn Cove Viaduct**
Visitor Center

TENNESSEE

RAINER GAP

Grandfather
Mountain
State Park

Beacon Heights

PISGAH

NATIONAL

FOREST

LENOIR

ELK PARK

LINVILLE

Wet Rock

310

NEWLAND

CROSSNORE

**NORTH CAROLINA**

ELIZABETHTON

**Linville Falls**
Visitor Center

MORGANTON

OAK HILL

CHEROKEE
NATIONAL
FOREST

LINVILLE FALLS

Table Rock Mountain

320

Chestoa View

JOHNSON
CITY

River Dam

Lake James
State Park

SPRUCE
PINE

BAKERSVILLE

330

McKinney Gap

Gillespie Gap

**Museum of
North Carolina**

**Credit: National Parks Service**

North Carolina

**Minerals**
Visitor Center

**Crabtree Falls**

ERWIN
MICAVILLE
SPRUCE PINE
MARION

BURNSVILLE

Mount Mitchell
(highest peak east of
the Mississippi River)

PISGAH

NATIONAL

Mount Mitchell
State Park

OLD FORT

FOREST

Rock Mountain Gap

Woolomine Falls Overlook

Graybeard Mountain Overlook

Craggy Dome Overlook

**Craggy Gardens**
Visitor Center

BLACK MOUNTAIN

MARSHILL

Z.B. Vance
Birthplace

Lake Tahkala
Overlook

CHIMNEY
ROCK

Bull Gap

SWANNANOA

BAT CAVE

Chimney Rock
State Park

WEAVERVILLE

Craven Gap

**Folk Art Center**

**Blue Ridge Parkway**
Visitor Center
and Park Headquarters

HOT SPRINGS

ASHEVILLE

Biltmore
Estate

SKYLAND

Spartanburg

Lake
Powhatan

The
North Carolina
Arboretum

MOUNTAIN
HOME

HENDERSONVILLE

PISGAH

NEWFOUND MOUNTAIN

MILLS RIVER

Carl Sandburg
Home National
Historic Site

NATIONAL

Elk Pasture Gap

CANTON

PISGAH NATIONAL FOREST

FOREST

Mount Pisgah

**Mt. Pisgah**

Wagon Road Gap

DuPont State
Recreational
Forest

Cradle of Forestry
in America

Cherry Cove Overlook

Young Pine

BREVARD

WAYNESVILLE

Graveyard Fields

Looking
Glass
Rock

Davidson
River

Graveyard
Ridge

Pisgah Center
For Wildlife
Education

GREAT SMOKY

MAGGIE
VALLEY

Heintooga
Overlook

Balsam Mountain

Devils
Courthouse

MOUNTAINS

Soco Gap

Highest Point on
Parkway 6053

NATIONAL PARK

CHEROKEE INDIAN
RESERVATION

**Waterrock Knob**
Visitor Center

Oconaluftee
Visitor Center

SYLVA

Southern End of
Blue Ridge Parkway
Milepost 469

CHEROKEE

NANTAHALA NATIONAL FOREST

SOUTH
CAROLINA

CASHIERS

BRYSON CITY

Overmountain Victory
National Historic Trail
American Revolutionary patriots
crossed the mountains in 1780
to defeat British loyalists at
Kings Mountain, South Carolina

MARION

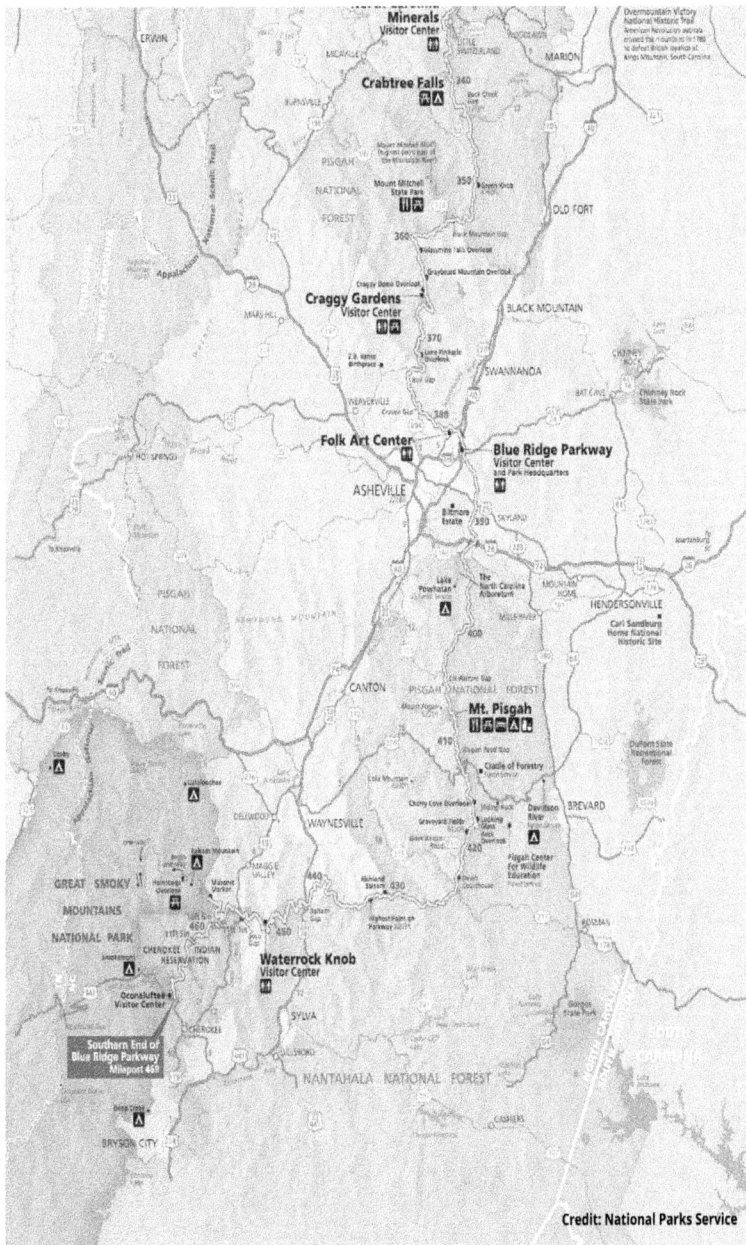

# Before the Ride

E ight months before Scott and I biked the Blue Ridge Parkway, the two of us met at Cameron Boys Camp. We both live here and disciple at-risk boys year-round. This isn't any old camp. The boys choose to come, work on their problems, and take some crazy adventures while they're here. They do all this in an outdoor setting – we live outside. We build our own little village in the wood out of the tall pine trees nearby. All this is done without power tools. We live a fairly primitive life, though we do have running water in our campsites. We cook for ourselves two days a week. The other five days we eat at our dining hall with the other groups. And we also have an indoor shower that we use, especially during winter. The campsite shower would be freezing half the year.

I hate to call what Scott and I do, work. It's really just living life with the boys and helping them overcome difficulties that have come their way. When I got to camp in 2009, I thought I found the perfect job. It incorporated my passions: youth, mission work, and adventure. I consider counselors at camp as domestic missionaries. What we do can be extremely difficult at times, but it's totally worth all the hardship to help change a boy's trajectory in life. During a boy's time at camp, he gets to build part of his campsite, accomplish goals he's written for himself, and, more often than not, catch up in school.

Most of the boys are behind when they come to camp. This isn't because they're dumb. Sometimes traditional school isn't geared for someone who has to sit in a classroom all day. Sometimes past trauma a boy hasn't dealt with prevents him from learning like he should. At camp everything is educational, even taking month-long hiking and canoe trips. The boys research and plan everything as a group. It gets checked to make sure it's safe and feasible, and then, the supervisors say, "Go have fun!" I could talk about camp for many more pages, but this ride didn't happen at camp.

Both Scott and I love taking adventures outside of camp too. This year, for our week-long summer break, we decided to bike the Blue Ridge Parkway. We usually have a nine-day break when the boys go home for an extended home visit to put into practice what they're learning with their families.

We chose the parkway in part, because of its difficulty. The parkway is a scenic highway running four-hundred, sixty-nine miles through the Appalachian Mountains of Virginia and North Carolina. It's actually an elongated park run by the National Parks Service with thousands of visitors, especially when fall foliage is at its peak. It's the most visited park in the nation. Narrow lanes, marked by forty-five mile per hour speed limit signs, guide you through forests, gorgeous mountains, and beautiful waterfalls. Scores of pull-offs allow vehicle-bound tourists to stretch their legs and admire the surrounding topography.

When you're out and about, you'll understand why the Smoky Mountains are so aptly named. You'll see the earth's lungs, so divinely shaped like bronchioles and alveoli within our own lungs. And you'll be amiss if you don't track a little dirt into your car after hiking to a crystal-clear waterfall, getting so close you feel its spray on your cheeks.

The Appalachian Mountains are among the oldest mountain ranges on earth. At their highest, they were taller than the Himalayas, but they've eroded through the ages until they reached their current form, fit for Scott and me to traverse through. Some of the oldest rivers in the world carve their paths near the Appalachians like the French Broad River in North Carolina and New River in Virginia. Also, there's the Susquehanna River up North in Pennsylvania and New York. People have long called this area home as well. Projectile points signify Paleo-American presence throughout the region.

The vast, twenty-one-hundred-mile Appalachian Trail crosses the parkway a couple of times for through-hikers aiming to reach either Georgia or Maine. Another walkway, the Mountains-to-Sea Trail, meanders a huge swath of the North Carolina parkway before turning South and East to stay in the state.

All kinds of attractions dot the parkway. Several parks and campgrounds exist solely for parkway travelers. Waterfalls and trails are in abundance. The trails range from easy to strenuous. Museums share flora, fauna, and geology of the area, local folklore, the distinct music of the Appalachians, quilts, old-timey crafts, and so much more.

Scott and I trained on our days off, riding around the Southern Pines area as often as we could. I remember one instance we were going to ride fifty-miles around Moore County. We got lost and ended up doing over sixty miles. I remember being utterly exhausted. My tight-fitted bike shirt and shorts turned white with salt crystals. It was brutally hot, and I'd guzzled all my water. When we were gathering our directional bearings, someone stopped and gave us some Gatorade. It was a God-send for sure.

Scott didn't train at much as I was able to. His group at camp had taken a long canoe trip. Canoeing all day without much walking wouldn't set him up well for the ride. He didn't care though; he's extremely athletic and has the determination of a bulldozer. He runs a lot, and he trained as much as could before he left. His athleticism, even without training, will carry him farther than me. We were excited to push ourselves physically, and to see what the majestic Appalachian Mountains could show us.

I had gotten into road biking through a friend, Chris Boone. He set the world record for cycling the parkway in 29 hours and 36 minutes. Chris and I met a few months after I came to camp through a Baptist Children's Homes of North Carolina (BCH) event, where he was training to ride nearly the entire length of North Carolina from Murphy to Manteo to raise money. Cameron Boys Camp is a part of BCH, and one of the few camps within the Wilderness Road Therapeutic Camping Association. We represent one of a dozen camps dotted throughout the Eastern United States under WRTCA's affiliation.

Originally, the event was going to be a collaborative endeavor with several staff of the Children's Homes riding sections of the route, but the organization's insurance wouldn't allow it. Chris stepped in and said he would do it... all by himself. He nearly did too, but that's a different story.

The bikes purchased for the staff participating in ride before the insurance company nixed it were essentially unused. I bought one from someone who wasn't going to ride other than for the event. On this bike, I learned how to balance on thin tires, avoid potholes, and draft. Going fast excited me. I also loved the thrill of pushing my body as hard as I could.

But this bike wasn't the one I took on my journey. John Ramos, the man who helped recruit me to camp, had taken scores of adventures, and inspired my wanderlust. We've traveled to several foreign countries together and experienced all kinds of different cultures. Before we met, he took a cross country ride during a hiatus from camp several years ago. He graciously let me use his sturdier, touring bike he'd taken from coast to coast in the U.S.

John had panniers, racks, and all the gear I needed for the ride. Thankfully, I didn't have to buy them. I packed a few changes of clothes, toiletries, a journal and bible, my camera, phone and chargers, and enough food for breakfasts and lunches. I brought my sleeping bag and borrowed a single-person tent from camp. For a pillow, I'd use rolled-up clothes. I was set. All I need to do now is get on the road.

# Sequestered

*July 20*

———————～———————

My alarm startled me awake at 4:00 a.m. I'd been dreaming of biking near my childhood home of Springdale, Arkansas. Once jolted from my sleep, it didn't take long before my eyes adjusted to the lamplight. I dressed, loaded my gear in the car, strapped my bike to the rack on the trunk, and waited for Scott to do the same. It didn't take us long. We prepared everything the night before and were ready to go.

The two of us pulled away from the driveway of our counselor's lodge around 5:00 a.m. on our way to Lisa's house, twenty minutes north in Sanford. Lisa, the camp cook, offered to shuttle us to Virginia and take my blue 1998 Honda Accord back to camp. She overheard our plan to bike the Blue Ridge Parkway when Scott and I were talking about it in the kitchen several weeks ago. It was just a dream then, but it's finally turning into a reality.

Lisa kept me entertained as I drove four hours to Rockfish Gap, Virginia, the northern terminus of the Blue Ridge Parkway. We talked about food, the boys and activities at camp, and various adventures we'd each been on. Scott chimed in when he wasn't dozing off in the backseat.

While Scott was asleep, Lisa and I reminisced about the Ranger group when I was a counselor. I'm a groupwork supervisor now. She's been as camp longer than I have. Occasionally, my group prepared a meal with Lisa for the two other groups and office staff. She had a grand time showing us how to peel and cut and measure and stir. It was a whirlwind in the kitchen with up to thirteen people, but every time we got the meal done and everyone loved what we created.

When we got to Rockfish Gap, Scott and I unloaded our gear and posed for pictures at the parkway sign. It was a perfect day. The temperature was pleasant, and there were big puffy clouds covering part of the sky. Despite the clouds, everything was bright. Birds sang nearby, and we caught the scent of freshly cut grass. We didn't linger too long before staying goodbye so Lisa could make the trek back. Our bike journey began at 10:00 a.m.

Early on, I stopped several times to adjust my panniers, the little saddlebags on the back of the bike. They didn't feel secure to the bike rack. They seemed to be bouncing when I rode. I was unaware I had to hook the bottom of the bag to the frame. Before I made this realization, I lost my left pannier after I ran over a pothole. It wasn't even an hour after we began. That hole nearly caused a major catastrophe.

As I sped downhill, I didn't maneuver away from a deceptively deep hole. The bike and I jolted. I felt the pannier come off. I looked back to see my gear careening all over the road at thirty miles per hour. Pummeling toward another crater, I looked forward just in time to stay upright. Braking hard, I pulled over to the side of the road and walked uphill to collect my gear. Somehow, I had gotten a little ahead of Scott. I finished picking up everything about the same time Scott rode up. He was unaware of my near-death experience.

He helped secure my bags, and I told him how close I was to disaster. Thankfully, my phone wasn't in the bag that went tumbling. However, my brand-new camera was. I'd gotten an Olympus Stylus Tough camera, one that's waterproof and supposedly crush and drop proof. Its only injuries were a few dents as it careened across the parkway. It's a quality camera, well worth the investment.

My heels kept hitting the panniers after hooking them to the bottom of the rack. Even after I securely put my panniers back on, they still gave me trouble. Two hours into the ride, I realized my bags were on the wrong side. We were less than thirty miles into our journey. I hoped the rest of the ride wouldn't be this stressful. I was becoming more acutely aware that I didn't really know what I was doing. With my bags now on the correct side and my single-man tent strapped to the top of the rack, we were ready to continue.

Scott wasn't anticipating how taxing the climbs were going to be. He and his group of boys at Cameron Boys Camp canoed two-hundred and fifty miles on the Suwannee River in Florida right before the boys went home. Canoeing most of the day can atrophy the lower half of your body. His sea legs haven't quite regained their strength. Nonetheless, he's been taking these hills in stride; we're staying pretty close together. He's a beast for taking on this trip without much training. There's no doubt in my mind that we'll finish.

Soon after I flipped my panniers to the correct sides, my tire came within inches of a camouflage body of a small copperhead snake sunning itself on the edge of the pavement. I pedaled back to warn Scott, then took a picture from a distance. Venomous snakes aren't regularly seen where we work. Looking at its triangular head and slitted, cat-like eyes, I observed the reptile as a dangerous creature of beauty rather than a bad omen. I wondered if we'd see more wildlife on a bike than we would if we were to drive the parkway in a car. I imagined we would, and was excited about all we would see.

Periodically, we took breaks at overlook parking lots. Hordes of gnats swarmed our faces, invading our eyes, ears, and noses. Exhaustion bred apathy, and we let the gnats fly uncontested. Luckily, they didn't bite. Several times throughout the day, I wondered what I'd gotten myself in to.

The Blue Ridge Parkway has mile markers every mile. They're short, cement rectangles about four inches wide and two feet tall. The mile number is chiseled out a little bigger than the width of my thumb. Dark blue paint makes the number visually pop out. Since they mark each mile, it's interesting to see how quickly they pass when we go downhill and how excruciatingly slow and seemingly wide-spread they are when we pedal uphill.

I timed our miles on several occasions throughout the day since it was so easy to tell how far we'd gone. Frequently, I looked at my right wrist to record when we flew passed the cement markers. Since I'm left-handed, I wear my watch on my right. It feels natural for me. Most people wear it on their left because they're right-handed. I'm not sure I can call myself a true lefty though. I play basketball and throw with my right.

Sixty miles couldn't have come sooner. We arrived at 4:30 p.m. to an abandoned Otter Creek campsite, restaurant, and gift shop. Scott and I were confused. Why was the campground closed in the middle of the summer? As we walked around, we found a sign stating the site was closed until October. It must be closed until the foliage begins to show its colors. The next available campsite was down the parkway half an hour... half an hour by car.

Not wanting to travel twenty-six more miles to the next available campground, we chose to stay here against the advice of the Parks Services. Out of eyesight from the parking lot, we set up our tents. We found a bear-proof container to store our gear. Our bikes were hidden near the locked bathrooms. I checked for possible water sources, and walked around all the buildings hoping for a power outlet. Everything was locked and turned off.

A stream running through the property allowed us to rinse the salt off our bodies. Our eyebrows and where our sideburns would be, if we had them, had salt crystals from sweat running down our faces and evaporating. The stream was shallow, no more than a foot and a half deep. We sat down in the water and took bird baths, flipping water over ourselves. A gentle cascade we could lean our backs against while sitting in the water served as our recliner when we were done. We stayed there quite a while letting the cool water soothe our muscles.

I noticed how tan my arms had already become. We didn't bring sunscreen. I can imagine the farmer's tan I'm going to have by the end of the trip. Usually, I either tan or I burn and the burn quickly fades into a tan. The contrast between the melanin-crazed skin and the skin hiding behind my bike shirt is surprising. While we were still in the water, I cleaned my shorts then draped them over the outside of my tent to dry. I crawled into my tent and closed my eyes for half an hour of blissful rest.

While Scott was still fast asleep in his own tent, I hopped back on my bike to search for cellphone service. Three or four miles into searching, I was able to send a text to my dad letting him know we'd made our mileage. Then, I sent Matthew a message. He was an old counselor at the camp whom I hadn't seen in a while. Matthew was a counselor in the middle group. Their ages were from twelve to fourteen. My old group, the Rangers, was the oldest. My boys ranged from fourteen to seventeen. We were never co-counselors, but we occasionally hung out if our days off lined up. Matthew lives twenty minutes away in Lynchburg. It'd be good to see him if he's available. A good meal and something to drink would be amazing too. Maybe he'll pay us a visit.

As soon as I sent the message, the thunder I'd been hearing all day materialized into a rainstorm. Speeding down the mountain, it was difficult to look up at the road in front of me with raindrops blasting me in the face. My hope was to return to Otter Creek before my unprotected phone became waterlogged and I'd be without a phone for the rest of the trip. Other than the anxiety of losing my phone, it was a fun ride. As soon as I got to the abandoned restaurant, I left the phone under the porch while I retrieved a Ziplock bag. I didn't want it to get even more wet as I ran to my tent. My bike jersey pocket kept it surprisingly dry, and it still worked.

All four of our water bottles are open catching rain. As I'm writing inside my tent, I'm fighting minor cramps while talking with Scott in the other tent. If it keeps raining, I may get unfiltered water from the stream. Expecting to be fed at the restaurant this evening, I resorted to Cliff Bars and flour tortillas for dinner. We only packed breakfasts and lunches so our bikes would be lighter. It would not be fun to eat cold meals three times a day. I guess we could have brought a camping stove and a small pot, but we didn't think that would be practical. Too much weight and bulk.

Sleep will come easy tonight.

9:21p.m.

# Banjos and Fireflies

*July 21*

———————⌇———————

A tough ascent from 650 feet to 3,950 feet in elevation in approximately fourteen miles welcomed us within the first hour of cycling. No downhills broke up the climb. We just kept climbing. I had my feet in the cages, so I was able to rest my normal pedaling muscles while I pulled the pedals up rather than pushing them down as I normally would.

Cages are the poor man's clips. Thin plastic strips surround the front half of my foot making a cage. Near the middle of my foot is a strap that cinches down so my foot stays in place. This allows me to pick up my foot to pedal as well as the traditional downward motion. It's also a little tricky to get out of them quickly because I have to bend over to each one to loosen the strap. Clips, on the other hand, are shoes that clip into an adapted pedal. I've never used them before, but I've heard they're much easier to get in and out of than cages.

The lack of water made the ride especially rough. This morning, I filled one water bottle in the creek hoping to fill my other at the James River Information Center a few miles down the road. Like Otter Creek, they were closed. Up and up and up the mountains we went. We stopped briefly at Apple Orchard Mountain. At 3950 feet, it's the highest point on the parkway in Virginia. Unfortunately, there aren't any apples there. I don't think it's the season for them anyway.

A middle-aged couple taking pictures at an overlook further down warned of a coyote hanging around the road. I doubted I'd catch sight of it, but a mile later I saw him staring at me before he ran into the cover of evergreen trees. He was an observant gray/white canine that watched as I approached his territory. I mused that I distracted him from hunting a rabbit or a field mouse. Or maybe he was just patrolling the area around his young litter who was hiding deeper in the evergreen grove. There's no way I would have been able to catch a glimpse if I weren't on my bike.

Twenty-five miles into our day, we stopped at Peaks of Otter, a fancy resort and restaurant. It was

11:00 a.m. We were the last table seated before it closed to prepare for lunch. I had high-calorie cheesy grits, two pancakes, and two scrambled eggs. Both Scott and I gulped several glasses of water before the waitress took our order. After eating, I put protein powder in my Gatorade bottle in the bathroom downstairs, hoping to drink it as an energy boost later in the day. Back on the road with a full stomach, I instantly felt much better. It's amazing what a good meal did for my energy level and demeanor.

It seemed like the rest of the ride went up and down. I liked this a lot more than the morning ride. The clouds were sparse in front of the great blue expanse, but they seemed to be piling up quickly. Overcast skies didn't bother me. It would help prevent sunburn. I wouldn't have to squint as much either.

About half an hour before we got to Mile Post 100, we stopped at an overlook for a quick break. There were a few old buggies there. The gentleman who owned a black one let us sit in the front for a picture. I didn't get the make and model. It was solid black, except the faux wooden spokes holding the thin tires that looked more like motorcycle tires than automobile tires. The sides were open air above the doors. A soft top was attached to the windshield, the only glass on the car. There was only enough room for the driver in the front, though two could have sat comfortably in the back. The gentleman's short-haired, labrador retriever smiled in the backseat with me as Scott took my picture.

At Mile Post 100, we initiated a six-mile descent. A duo of bikers headed north informed us of this luxury while at the restaurant. As soon as we passed the century post, the skies opened with fury. We briefly stopped to waterproof our panniers. I had extravagantly loud, yellow covers that came with the panniers John loaned me. They bungeed snugly to the outside of the bag, preventing rain to permeate my clothes inside. I could hardly see in front of me as water and wind rushed passed my face, hitting and rolling over my glasses. The potholes were huge, so I avoided them without much difficulty. We were going fast. I don't think it took us more than twelve or thirteen minutes to get down.

When we reached the end of our downhill, I stopped to take a picture of a green, cow-filled pasture. Pristine mountains in the background helped make the picture perfect. While waiting for me to take the shot, Scott stumbled upon a huge blackberry patch along the fence line. Most of them were red, but there were plenty of dark, ripe berries. We gorged ourselves in the downpour until the rain slowed to a drizzle. Fresh fruit was a treat. I could have scavenged every plump berry.

I had some trouble with my bike this afternoon. My gears wouldn't switch. Tired and frustrated, I struggled in a higher gear for fifteen minutes. Fed up, I slipped out of my cages, jumped off the bike, and manually moved the chain. I got grease all over my hands, but I didn't care. I was glad to be pedaling easier. A couple hills later at an overlook parking lot, a middle-aged, Good Samaritan gave me a bottle of cold water. The gentleman sitting inside the gold van with his wife said he rarely buys water. It must have been a miracle. My bottles weren't empty yet, but I wanted to conserve what I had. I drank half and sat the bottle on the ground for Scott.

His wife gave me a wet wipe and told me to clean my face. Inadvertently, I'd gotten grease all over myself, wiping sweat off my brow and nose. I was mildly embarrassed, but I also embraced the grease as warpaint and a badge of hard-earned success. I thanked them both for their gifts. Scott and I shared a little of our journey before we parted ways.

We're staying at Roanoke Mountain Campground tonight. It, too, is permanently closed for camping due to seasonal sequesters. I didn't realize most of the visitors to the Blue Ridge Parkway came in the fall, when the leaves on the trees explode with color. I've been in this area before and was able to see the innumerable hues the leaves show off. Valleys look like bowls of fruit loops cereal. Each species of tree boasts its own unique spread of color. And each individual tree wears their colors just a little bit different based on sun exposure and temperature. It's quite mesmerizing because it's so different than what'd you see any other time of the year.

Despite being closed, the campground wasn't vacant. Bill Thompson, the camp host seemed to recognize our plight and let us stay. He showed us a secluded area to pitch our tents. There would be a lot of people here tonight. The campground would be hosting a bluegrass concert, and he didn't want anyone knowing we were staying the night.

Dropping our gear off deep in the primitive camping section, we asked Bill for directions to town and rode three miles to Roanoke. There, we found a burger and pizza joint called Fork in the Alley. I ordered a burger and also split a pizza with Scott. While eating, I looked at the storm system we went through this afternoon on my phone's weather app. It was intense. Going that fast soaking wet chilled me faster than I anticipated, especially when we got to the campsite and weren't riding anymore. Tired and still cold even though we were in dry clothes now, we thought it best to get back to camp.

We found a shortcut online to the campground, and opted to save a few minutes. What we thought was a normal intersection on the map turned out to be a bridge with no way down to the road below. The very one we needed to take to the campground. We tried to see if it connected somewhere else but it didn't. We had to backtrack to the bridge and carry our bikes down the hill. It probably evened itself out timewise, though I'm holding on to the assumption that is was shorter than our original route. We coasted through the park's gate and hid our bikes as concert-goers began walking to the three-walled lean-to for the show carrying lawn chairs.

Scott and I were the youngest bluegrass concert attendees by far, like thirty years younger. Reclining on a grassy knob, we listened to the quintet on stage. A fiddle, an acoustic guitar, a banjo, a cello, and some sort of dulcimer a lady was plucking while standing up provided the entertainment tonight. I didn't know many of the songs, but the sound surrounding us on that little knob was soothing. Also, in my mind, bluegrass is quintessential music of the Appalachian Mountains. I love the twang. It's almost foreign from modern pop music; it has soul. I believe the soul I was listening to tonight was exuding from the people playing the instruments. Just like my dad taught me to answer the phone with a smile because he said the person on the other side of the line can notice a happier tone in your voice, I think the soulful music comes from the character of the one creating the music. They love what they do.

Laying on the grass with the music in the background, I closed my eyes and replayed the day's events. The dance floor caught my attention as soon as I opened my eyes. I paused my thoughts to record the scene. The dance area was a tiny wooden floor laid out on the freshly-cut grass. It couldn't be more than ten feet by ten feet. No one had used it yet. As soon as this particular song began, a few white-haired ladies bounced out of their lawn chairs and made their way to the tiny floor.

A thick-builded, old man wearing jean shorts and a blue t-shirt slowly made his way over. As soon as he hit the wooden planks, he transformed into a teenager. The mountain music must have beckoned him to a time long ago. His feet moved wildly to and fro, in sync with the music. The old man was captivating. Never have I seen such joy emitting from a concert of elderly folks. On and on he went, without slowing down. Eight were up there cutting loose now. All but two were well into their sixties.

When the music faded, old man stepped off the platform, back into his aged body. His posture, his spryness, vanished when his shoes hit the grass. Hobbling back to his lawn chair, I wondered what was going through his mind. Were his thoughts still swirling around days of old? Was he lamenting the state of his life now or was he happily satisfied?

I didn't see anyone leave early. The two-hundred in attendance stayed until the last song was played, Amazing Grace. Everyone stood up from their multi-colored lawn chairs to sing the first, third, and fourth verses.

Scott and I went to bed after everyone left. It was dark by then, and the glow of hundreds of fireflies blinking their bioluminescent rear ends lulled us to sleep. I laughed to myself remembering what I learned at a museum with my group at camp: the sole purpose of the firefly's light is to attract a mate.

# Miracle On a Century

*July 22*

———————————⌇———————————

We left Roanoke Mountain Campground at 6:45 a.m. this morning, waving goodbye to Bill from his mobile home. Last night, he told us to leave a little before 7:00 a.m. A park ranger would be making his rounds at that time and none of us were sure what he'd do if he learned that we spent the night here. We didn't want to get Bill into any trouble. His generosity saved our evening last night. It would have been drastically less pleasurable somewhere else.

Moderately rolling hills inaugurated our third morning on the road. A few sections of these hills had steep grades, but they weren't too bad. Sometimes it's difficult to appreciate the beauty around me when I'm going uphill. Most of the time

I'm either looking down at my feet or straight ahead trying to calculate how far up I have left to go. Stretches of descents came shortly after the steep climbs, making our journey more enjoyable, but they wouldn't last.

About midmorning, I saw a deer grazing by the side of the road. The buck was unaware of me until the last minute when he picked his head up and spooked. He took off in the same direction I was going. Running beside me for twenty yards, he looked as if he was going to dart right in front of me. I covered my brakes with both hands, hoping we didn't collide if he decided to cross the road. But no, the buck bolted off to the West, into the woods. Scott saw the whole thing and said he wished I would have jumped off my bike onto the deer. That would have been a crazy story.

For lunch, we ate at a quaint café in Mabry Mill on the East side of the parkway. One hundred-seventy-six miles were behind us. The café was four miles shy of our halfway point for the day. We passed the old Mabry family gristmill right before we got to the café, which sat in the rear of a souvenir store. The waitress walked Scott and me to the seating area, a long narrow sunroom with several ceiling fans. The room had crème-colored walls and a large window where workers could bus drinks and food.

Pancakes, cheesy grits, and an egg appealed to my appetite again. This time the restaurant had sweet potato pancakes. I'm allergic to regular, white potatoes; it has something to do with the starch. I've heard regular white potatoes are roots, while sweet potatoes are tubers. I don't quite know what the difference is. All I know is that I'm able to eat sweet potatoes, and I love them. Both of us enjoyed our meals, taking our time to savor each bite. There was no need to rush.

On the road again, I kept my mind occupied by breathing in rhythm. 1 - 2 - 3 in, 1 - 2 out. Three counts in and two counts out. My breaths were in sync with my pedaling. Chris taught me this little trick. By syncing my breathing to my pedaling, I would alternate exhales on a different foot each cycle, making myself less likely to get a cramp in one of my sides. Ever since Chris showed me this technique, I've been using it when I run too.

I had plenty of time to think, but the majority of my time was spent breathing and absorbing the beauty around every turn. The air smelled fresh and pure. Looking wide, the expanse of lush green trees against the brilliant blue and cloud-white sky was picturesque, but not in a way that would win any photography contests. The cluttered sky was moving with clouds. Trees grew as they wished. I could see them for miles along the mountains.

Some of the trees were straight, reaching for the sun. Others were gnarled and broken or burled with cancer. The imperfect ones close to the road caught my attention. Something must have happened to disrupt the tree's growth. Was it heavy ice that bent its trunk or a neighboring tree that fell? Did insects bore into the tree causing it to writhe and grow differently? Did a deer munch on the terminal bud of a young pine, causing a limb to turn toward the heavens and become the new trunk? I had no idea what story each tree could tell. I only knew that every one of them seemed to value life and worked toward the best life it could have. Trees can teach volumes if we pay attention.

Looking closer around me, I noticed hundreds of baby blue chicory flowers that dotted a sprawling clover blanket. The blue against the green was like the inverse of the rich, blue sky and the trees above. Other than the road, I couldn't see anything else man-made. The whole earth was alive, growing and moving and accomplishing its purpose. An elegance of natural, living goodness. I was seeing all this in high definition. I had time to make the many connections that this glimpse of Eden was honoring its Creator.

At mile two-hundred-thirteen, we made a detour at the Music Museum near Galax, Virginia, five minutes before its five o'clock closing. Water had been scarce, and we found a cold, refreshing supply here. The front attendant brought out an elevation map of the parkway to his desk. He made sure to highlight an enormous vertical accent close to the conclusion of the parkway. As he talked, worry crept into my mind. I envisioned a straight road with no turns. I could see exactly how far I had to go up. I pedaled and pedaled until I went so slow that I would fall over if I didn't hop off. It may seem strange, but I want to be able to say I pedaled every step of the way without having to walk my bike. I don't want my vision to come true, especially so close to the end.

The attendant noted there was no place to eat in Doughton Park. The town of Galax was the closest option, seven miles off the parkway. I knew it was wise to eat and suggested we hitch to town for a meal because neither of us really wanted an extra fourteen miles. Scott mildly opposed the idea, but, as always, we stayed unified throughout all our decisions.

With thumbs in the air, we decided to give it a try. No one stopped. None. I figured being in the middle of nowhere, some country gentleman with a truck would pull over who'd be able to tote us and our bikes to town. Several people passed us, but no one stopped. Discouragement began to creep over us. We kept smiling as cars passed us wondering if we were going to eat tonight.

We donned our helmets to make it blatantly obvious we were bikers. Back at Cameron Boys Camp when we take the groups on canoe trips, we ask the counselors and the boys to keep their lifejackets on if they need to ask for help or knock on a door for water. I've learned through experience that people are a lot more likely to help if you're wearing a lifejacket. I thought the same would happen with our bike attire. The lack of hospitality surprised me. Even with lifejackets, no one came to our aid.

Scott thought of deliver-ordering pizza to the park. It was a brilliant idea. I had cell service and looked up all the pizzerias nearby. The second shop informed us that no one in the entire county delivered. I was a little surprised by this too. How can no pizzeria around here offer delivery? It seemed like tonight's meal will echo our first night's meal.

On we went. Stopping at the Mile Post 220 sign, we each posed for pictures. This was special because it represented one hundred miles today. A century on a bike has been on my bucket list for a while. Now I'll be able to check it off. With over fifty tasks categorized into different sessions, my bucket list is pretty extensive. Some of the categories are: travel, see, experience, educational, physical/skill, and philanthropy. For example: I want to travel to Hawaii, see the African migration, make mud bricks, take a class on the Ancient Near East, walk twenty miles in a day, and volunteer at a hospital. This one-hundred-mile bike ride in a day crosses off something in my physical/skill category.

One hundred, twenty miles was on today's itinerary. Around Mile Post 230, we began ascending. A sign showed the elevation at 2,800 feet. I knew we were in for a few climbs to finish out the day's ride. Air Bellows Gap, which is 3,700 feet, is close to the park.

We shared with each other the burden of our sore and aching bodies, but never complained. When one of us matter-of-factly stated we were thirsty or cramping or exhausted we were merely vocalizing our mutual suffering. It was never meant to draw pity to ourselves or subtly whine about the journey we were on. This shared trial brought each of us peace and power.

The last five or six miles were in thick mist. Occasionally, we'd ride up over the clouds and see green islands of other peaks that were above the cloud-line. Time crept slowly. I was exhausted. There was nothing more I wanted to do but crawl into my sleeping back and go to sleep. I had given up hope for a meal. I was so tired that I was content going to bed hungry. As the miles rolled on I kept looking for the brown metal sign that signified the end of our ride.

Finally, Scott and I made it to Doughton Park. Our monstrous day was complete! It was a little after 8:00 p.m. when we unload of bikes and set up tents. Caloric and timely efficiency was our priority tonight. We wanted to get in bed and forget our aching legs and stomachs, while expending the least amount of energy possible. The last thing to do was hit the bathroom and get some water.

Darkness was already pulling its veil over the sky when I walked across the grass to the bathroom with Scott. A lady camping nearby asked if we needed anything to eat. What did she just say? Bewilderment and joy displayed themselves as childish grins on our faces when we heard those words. We replied with a fervent, "Yes!" She asked what we'd like to eat. I blurted the first thing that popped into my head, "Carbs or anything you have". She laughed and waved us over. I couldn't believe we were going to eat tonight!

We waited with her husband, Jim, as Susan perused the trunk of her car. The couple were on the last day of their three-week traveling adventure and had a lot of food left over. She fired up the camp stove and prepared a boxed pasta meal for us. It was complimented with bread and little snack packs. It was the perfect meal for us. As Scott and I ate, we told them what we were doing, and tried to convey that we weren't grossly underprepared; we just weren't expecting so many closures along the parkway. They seemed to understand. They didn't pass any judgement on us. It felt like their only intention was to serve.

Rain began to fall as we got our post-dinner tea, so we gulped it down and said hurried goodbyes, promising to talk more with them in the morning. There's no doubt God orchestrated a magnificent blessing through Jim and Susan.

# Biking Legs

*July 23*

————————⟨∼⟩————————

Jim and Susan were already up and about when we woke up. We noticed them packing as we rolled up our tents. We packed everything up the same way we've done the last few days. I put a few snacks in my back pocket for later this morning and refilled my water bottle. When our morning routine was complete, we walked toward the friendly couple.

Jim wore glasses, a ball cap, and a short, white beard. He was about three inches taller than me. His thick, strong hands shook mine as I conveyed my appreciation once again. Susan was preparing oatmeal on the camp stove. Her smile brightened our morning. Shorter than her husband by eight inches or so, Susan had short, golden hair and also had glasses. You would tell they'd done their fair share of traveling. Both had cream-colored shirts with animals on them. Jim had an alligator; Susan, some sort of egret or heron.

Scott and I were treated to oatmeal and grain-filled bread. The bread was thick. It tasted and even smelled nutritious unlike plain, white bread I can't stand. Eating on the edge where the parking lot met the curb, we learned Jim worked for the park service in Florida. Susan taught at a local school. Before moving South, the couple lived in Indiana. While they lived in Indiana, they bicycled all the way to Florida, then cycled their way to Maine. They've pedaled probably thousands of miles over the years. I couldn't believe we were being taken care of by two cyclists! Their journeys were much more epic than ours.

They knew just how it felt to be hungry on the road; how it felt to wish for level ground around the next turn. They said as soon as you get your blood sugar up, even with a small cookie or handful of raisins, your mood instantly lifts and your legs don't feel like fifty-pound weights. We knew the feeling well. Jim said even in his prime, when he was biking thirty years ago, he wouldn't have done the parkway. We took that as quite the compliment.

Scott and I told them about some of the trips we'd been on at Cameron Boys Camp. He relayed stories about his most recent Suwannee River canoe trip in Florida. I told some of the events on the Ocmulgee and Altamaha Rivers when my group went last year in Georgia and the Green River trip we took in Kentucky. The four of us told stories of nature and roughing it and being blessed to take the adventures we had.

Time flew. Jim and Susan were easy to talk with, and we marveled at the adventures they took so long ago. They obviously didn't lose their sense of adventure and love for nature. Everything they needed for their three-week trip was packed away in their car: tent, food, everything. I hope that sense of adventure never escapes me either.

We finally finished breakfast together well after our bowls were empty. They wanted to get on the road. So did we. They had a long drive ahead of them. We made sure they knew how thankful we were for asking about us last night. Their kindness will be etched in my mind forever. I still can't believe we were taken care of by two bikers. After we exchanged contact information, they wished us well and we went our separate ways. We got on the road a little later than usual, but that didn't matter. It was worth all the time in the world.

Biking this morning felt much easier than the previous days. I think I'm finally getting my biking legs. When the groups at camp go on canoe trips, we tell the boys they'll get canoe arms after a few days of paddling. It takes some time for your muscles to build strength and stamina. It appears the same is true for biking.

Today, I realized the magnitude air current and momentum can have while I'm riding. Every bit counts, from leaning over the front wheel to tucking my knees and elbows. I learned that when the road leveled out, I could keep a fast pace for miles if I'd just come off a downhill. If I'd just climbed, I would drudge, even when on level ground.

On one of the long climbs, my chain popped off as I switched to a lower gear. Tired, but going fast enough to stay balanced, I was able to maneuver it back in gear without jumping off. I wasn't sure I could do it, but it was a fun challenge. I don't have clips or special shoes, just the cages with straps that tighten around my running shoes. I'd gotten used to slipping in and out of the cages, so I imagine that helped me be able to get the chain back on the crankset without falling over.

We stopped at Jumpinoff Rock and leaned our bikes against a picnic table. A round-trip hike to the viewpoint was only a mile. The vista was similar to what we've seen along the parkway, but it felt good to stretch our legs. I don't think we've gotten numb to the parkway's beauty, but rather we were expecting something spectacular due to having to hike for a view. Shortly after we left, we saw several highland cows grazing in a freshly mowed field. Those cows have a long tuft of hair between their huge horns. I snapped a picture of one with the blue mountains in the background.

We made another stop at E.B. Jeffress Park around mile two-hundred, seventy-two. The Cascades Trail was in our sights, after we filled our water bottles in the bathroom. I wasn't expecting much due to the view from our last detour, but this hike was totally worth it. The falls looked like a bubbling, white road descending into the lush green forest. The watery road was narrow, with all kinds of plants trying to encroach on the cascade but were beaten back. Mountain laurel and rhododendron were common along the trail. Both look similar to each other. They're evergreen bushes with big, waxy leaves. The distinguishing characteristics, at least to me, are the thickness of their leaves and their flowers. The mountain laurel has smaller, white clusters of flowers, and I believe the rhododendron has big, pink clusters of flowers.

It took thirty minutes for us to return to the starting point after seeing the cascade. On the way back, I found a blueberry bush with two tiny berries.

Wild blueberries are smaller and sweeter than store-bought berries. It was a cool little find. Scott and I were thankful to have one a-piece.

Almost immediately after we got back on our bikes, we stopped at the Tompkins Knob Overlook. It had an interesting replica cabin that lent itself as a church for traveling preachers back in the day. The sign said most of the services were held outdoors and the cabin was more of an inn or parsonage for the preachers who would come and go. We didn't spend too much time here and kept heading South on the parkway.

On this trip, I had a goal to go over the speed limit. A roommate in college was into biking way before I was. He told me a story about going over the speed limit on one of his rides. For some reason that fascinated me, and I wanted to do that too. The parkway's limit is forty-five miles per hour the whole way, but I thought I could do it under the right circumstances.

I knew the only way I could hit higher than forty-five was on a steep downhill. Switching to my highest gear, I forced my feet down on their pedals as hard as I could. I crouched low, glancing at my bike computer. I was in the forties. Any wobble or unforeseen pothole would end this trip. I kept pedaling with as much force as I could. Forty-seven showed on the little screen. Wind whipped across my face as I covered my brakes and began coasting. The thrill of speeding down the mountain, boosted my mood. Whew, that was fun!

For an early dinner, we stopped at a tavern in Blowing Rock, North Carolina less than five miles from Julian Price Campground, our stopping point for the day. We parked our bikes on the side of the building and walked up the steps. I ordered a colossal plate of nachos and a chicken tender meal. Scott ordered the same nacho meal and an appetizer of fried macaroni and cheese. I didn't feel bad with eating two entrées every night we could. Before the ride, Chris told us to eat whatever we needed. We'd be so calorie deficient that anything we ate would just be turned into fuel. He said the more we ate, the better.

I called Chris from the restaurant to give him an update on where we were. He suggested we come to his place tonight, but I thought it better to wait until tomorrow. Grandfather Mountain is close to Julian Price. We want to see that before traveling down to see Chris. I've heard we have to cross a wobbly, wooden bridge to get to the top. It's supposed to be one of the highest swinging bridges in the United States. We coordinated a plan for tomorrow, and I kept munching away at my food.

Unable to finish my meals, I asked for a bag for the spare tenders. Rather than throw them away, I wanted to use these to supplement my breakfast or lunch tomorrow. Scott and I had already buckled our helmets when our waitress ran down the stairs, waving at us. She held Scott's credit card between her fingers. That was close.

Arriving at our destination for the evening with plenty of time to spare, we rode around to scope out a good campsite. On the East side of the park was the lake. Wanting a less crowded area, we chose to camp away from the lake on the other side of the parkway. We set up our tents. I organized my food, clothes, and other gear in my panniers.

When we were done, Scott went for a prayer walk. I went to the welcome station to journal and charge my phone. A mother and daughter who spoke French, joined me to charge their phone and computer. I thought it was a little unusual hearing another language on the parkway, but then again, this is a big tourist destination. I suspected they were from Canada. The pair had a difficult time getting the universal adapter to fit the plug. I wasn't able to help as much as I would have liked, but they were eventually able to charge the daughter's phone.

Surrounded by trees, we ended the day full, happy, and peacefully.

# Home-cooked Meal

*July 24*

———————～———————

Our night at Julian Price was pleasant and uneventful. We packed up this morning with no rush to get started. With all my gear freshly organized from last night, it was a breeze. Everything in my panniers always goes in the same place. It's easier for me to pack it that way. And if I have to stop for a snack or to take a picture, it doesn't take any time to get what I want out because I've memorized its location. I wrapped a chicken tender from last night in a tortilla and stuck it in my rear shirt pocket for a midmorning snack. Some bike shirts have a pocket in the back middle of the shirt for food, a phone, or whatever.

We saw the Linn Cove Viaduct well before we reached it on the curvy parkway. A viaduct is a specific type of bridge. I had no idea what it was before today. This one follows the contours of the mountain and was built to reduce the road's impact on the environment around Grandfather Mountain. I appreciate that the engineers didn't destroy the habit around the parkway for this section. As much as humans can work with nature the better.

As we approached the viaduct, we began going downhill. I was nearing twenty miles per hour when a gust of wind blasted me in the face. Instantly, I slowed to a crawl. It was as if a gale had just hit the loose sails of a ship, stopping her in her tracks. Before getting hit, I stopped pedaling and was coasting with my head down and knees tucked. Now, I had to regain some of my momentum and began working again.

Scott saw me slow down and thought it was odd that I'd nearly grind to a halt. He wondered if I saw something in the road. A few seconds later the wind hit him, and it all made sense. We're a lot more vulnerable to the elements on a bike. Wind, sun, temperature, rain all have a greater effect on us, but oddly enough, I like it that way. It means I'm less in control and there's more adventure... more unknown that I have to endure or adapt to.

We stopped at the Linn Cove Viaduct Visitor Center just before opening. Since we couldn't go in yet we took a trail, called the Tanawha Trail, that meandered under the viaduct. We hiked to the thick cement braces for the bridge but turned around before we reached a good viewpoint. We returned to see an employee hoisting the American flag. We walked through the museum quickly then went on our way. Before leaving, the gentleman at the flagpole instructed us to not miss the Grandfather Mountain Entrance a mile off the parkway. We thanked him and hopped back on our bikes.

It didn't take long for us to reach our next point of interest. Once we arrived at Grandfather Mountain, we were told that bikes weren't allowed and the entrance fee was eighteen dollars. We thought about leaving our bikes at the bottom and hitchhiking to the top, but decided to forgo the idea. Bummed, we turned around, got back on the parkway, and continued fourteen or fifteen miles to Linville Falls. I'd been to Linville Falls before and knew it didn't have an entrance fee.

As we rode up to the Linville Falls Visitor Center we saw two cyclists. They had sleeping bags and tents on the back of their bikes, just like us. Sharing the commonality of cycling, we struck up a conversation and learned they traveled from Greensboro to Ashville, and had come here on their way to their next destination, whatever that was. They weren't doing the entire parkway like we were. The two guys were on their way out as we rode up, so we kept the conversation short so they could get going.

We hiked to the lower falls first. I realized how much I don't like walking downhill. Walking up hurts my muscles; down hurts my joints. A father and daughter were on their way down with us, making only four at the bottom to view the falls. They left shortly after reaching the bottom, so Scott and I had it all to ourselves. We sat on a boulder with water undercutting the bottom on its way downstream. He took a siesta in the sunshine, while I explored the area, getting a closer view of the falls.

I can't remember how long I explored. It was good to use my legs in a different capacity. Wandering through the woods is one of my favorite things. Soft ground underneath my feet, the smell of the leaves, birds and bugs singing, all seemed to detox me further from the modern world than this bike trip already has. This spot also has the chorus of water falling. Believe it or not, I've heard waterfalls can create negative ions in the air, which can increase blood flow to the brain and act as antidepressants. Just another benefit of being out in nature.

Thinking Scott left without me, I began walking toward the trail. When I got within eyesight of the boulder he was sleeping on, I found him behind it, washing off. I waited him to finish then we hiked back to the visitor center. There, we decided to go to the other trail on the other side of the visitor center to get another perspective of the falls. This was the high view, way above the place we just were. We didn't stay long at the top. I liked the lower part best because we were closer to the water.

I sent Chris a text at 12:20 p.m. from where we left out bikes near the visitor center, informing him we were on our way to Spruce Pine. It would be between ten and fifteen miles until we stopped for the day at the Mineral Museum, our rendezvous point. He was going to pick us up here and we'd go fifteen miles north to Bakersville, where he lives. Today is very light on miles compared to a couple days ago.

My knee started hurting last part of the ride, making the final section long and uncomfortable. We made it to the museum and coasted off the parkway and into the parking lot. Chris was busy on a job, and called to say his sister would pick us up.

We spent our time walking through the exhibit. I didn't realize mica was used in all kinds of electronics and is mined heavily around here. Mica is a silvery, shiny mineral. It's found at camp too. We've found big chunks that flake off in ultra-thin sheets when the boys were rambling around in the woods.

We reclined on the wooden bench outside after we walked around a little. I don't think anyone else was there. I just wanted to sit and do nothing. Half an hour later, both of us raised our heads to a friendly voice asking for two tired bikers.

Teresa helped us load our bikes into her old work truck and took us to Chris's house. He was there working on a bike. The yellow road bike was getting new brakes and a rear cassette. Chris was selling it to help fund his anniversary getaway next week. We sat on the couch and relaxed, watching the news while he worked. It was good to see him. We hadn't seen each other in a while. The three of us talked about biking, what God was doing in our lives, and what Scott and I would see further down the parkway.

Lisa, Chris's wife, made vegan lasagna for dinner. The four of us and their son, Zach, sat at the dining room table for our meal. As we dug in, I was confused when I noticed that the lasagna had cheese on top. I asked Lisa about this. Chris piped up and said it was from a vegan cow. I tried not to laugh and refocused my concentration on Lisa as she told us the cheese was made from soy. I liked it and couldn't taste the difference between it and real cheese. Vegetables from the farmer's market made up two side dishes. Scott and I finished the rest of the lasagna and nibbled on the veggies. I appreciated their attention to good health and supporting local farmers. All three are machines. Chris's forte is cycling, Zach runs a sub-4:30 mile, and Lisa does all kinds of fitness programs.

Chris and his family went to deliver the newly fixed, yellow bicycle to its new owner. Right after they returned from the delivery Lisa and Zach went to their church down the road. Chris, Scott, and I went to Ingles grocery store to stock up on Cliff Bars and other necessities. All of us bought a drink at Starbucks inside the grocery. I got a white chocolate mocha frapachino, my go-to drink there. It's rare when I go, but we felt we deserved a treat. Chris got his usual, venti green tea. I can't remember what Scott ordered. For being kind of in the middle of nowhere this Ingles had everything.

After returning to Chris's home, we put in season two of Duck Dynasty. This was my first time watching the show. It's a fun comedy; something mindless that offered a break from reality. Normally I'm not an over-the-top ridiculous comedy kind of guy but tonight, I didn't care. Scott and I watched a couple episodes with the family before they went to bed. We hit the sack shortly afterward, unrolling our sleeping bags in the living room.

# Minefield

*July 25*

─────────────── ⌇ ───────────────

This morning I woke to find Scott on a deflated mattress. He didn't care. He said it was warmer and more comfortable than what he'd been sleeping on the last several days. Everyone in the Boone home had already left for the day when we got up. We waited around the house for Teresa. She took us to meet Chris at DT's Blue Ridge Java in Spruce Pine. This is one of his favorite spots for breakfast. I love local restaurants way more than chains. As much as I can, especially when I'm traveling, I go out of my way to avoid well-known eateries.

At DT's, I had Cutler's Calamity, which boasted a bagel with cheese, crème cheese, chives, and bacon. It was delectable! Scott got the same. He liked it so much, he went back for a second. I also ordered two mini chicken sandwiches, and saved one for the road.

Chris had something unexpected come up at work he needed to take care of, so he left early. Teresa took us back to the Mineral Museum. Scott and I thanked her for her kindness and for being our chauffeur the last eighteen hours. Ready to start our next leg, we hopped on our bikes. We began a climb that seemed like miles and miles.

Before Scott and I started on the Blue Ridge Parkway, I told myself I wouldn't go under ten miles per hour. There were a few times this trip where I was close to single digits. I willed myself to keep my speed up during those uphill climbs. On the way up, I couldn't rest all the way or I'd go under my goal. Sucking wind, I'd finally reach the top.

I threw that out the window today. I was trying so hard on a long hill and saw nine on the computer. It probably happened to me on our high mileage day too, but I just wasn't looking. I was too tired to be frustrated; it was just a personal goal anyway. I was doing as well as I could. So much for my biking legs. Even though I went under ten miles per hour I was more determined not to walk.

My left knee was still bothering me from yesterday. I raised my seat twice at Chris's suggestion. He wanted my legs almost straight when my pedal was closest to the ground. It relieved most of the pain probably caused by hiking downhill at Linville Falls yesterday. I'm thankful for his wisdom.

Chris also informed me that I wasn't able to use all my gears. I'm using John's green, touring bike he took across the United States. Before Scott and I started our journey, I switched the seat and the wheels from John's bike with the wheels and seat on my road bike. My road tires are thinner than John's. I wanted to be more efficient on the road. My seat was more comfortable than his; that was an easy swap.

In addition to the tires being different, the other difference in the two rear wheels was the cassette. What I didn't know was that the rear cassette on my rear wheel had too many gears for the shifting mechanism on John's frame. I could only shift so far, leaving some of the gears out of reach and unused. Chris said it wasn't that big of a deal. There wasn't anything I could do about it anyway.

Near Mount Mitchell State Park, we saw signs indicating the parkway was closed. We looked at each other a little bewildered. Orange detour signs started appearing. The detour was an annoyance for someone in a vehicle. It would be compounded immensely for us on the bikes. The thought of a road closure never crossed our minds. This detour would have added tons of miles to our journey. And

I really wanted to say we biked the entire four-hundred and sixty-nine miles of the parkway. We didn't know what to do except to keep going and see what we could do when we got to the closure.

When we arrived to the closure near Mount Mitchell State Park, the large gates that we had seen periodically along the road were pulled shut. These gates are usually used in winter when large swaths of the parkway are closed due to snow and ice. This time they were shut for construction.

Several parked cars were here too. One was a park ranger's vehicle. We found him and asked what was going on. He informed us that the road had slipped a little downhill, but cyclists and pedestrians were allowed through. He let us through the gates! We were relieved. I'm extremely thankful we didn't have to take the detour. Those other cars parked near the closure... they were walkers and hikers taking advantage of a car-free parkway. We passed them the first couple miles of closed road. I didn't see any other cyclists.

Both Scott and I noticed once we got through the gates, the accumulated sticks and leaves on the road created hazards everywhere. I don't know how long cars weren't able to drive on this section, but I didn't realize vehicles either crush or blow the debris out of the way as much as they did. Leaves and sticks were everywhere. They probably covered half the road on some parts.

Meandering through the minefield, we made it to the Craggy Gardens Visitor Center located before the actual construction site responsible for the closure. It was deserted. The park service didn't turn off the water, and I jumped at the opportunity to fill both water bottles. The men's side was under construction so I went to the women's side. After using the restroom, I was surprised to hear Scott talking to a lady outside. Hurriedly, I made my way outside so I wouldn't be caught in an awkward situation if she came down the steps. I met them where I left Scott by the front door peering into the large, glass windows. During our five-minute conversation, we learned she started cycling from the opposite end of the closure and was planning to summit Mount Mitchell. She also helps lead a two-hundred- and forty-mile ride annually. We wished each other well, then parted ways.

A little farther South, we hopped off our bikes to observe the crack in the road. On the other end of the long crack, a team of workers took soil samples. Abundant rain had saturated the ground enough for the road to shift downhill. A two-hundred-foot crack, four inches wide and six feet deep ran right along the center yellow line. The crack split the two center lines almost perfectly. It was as if the road was a graham cracker and someone split it down the perforation. The East side of the road, which was facing downhill, was also deteriorating. We tipped our heads to the work crew and went on our way.

After cycling passed the crack, we descended to the Folk Art Center, dodging debris until cars were allowed back on the road. Inside the Folk Art Center, I purchased an *iBiked the Blue Ridge Parkway* sticker and asked if there were any restaurants close by. Ole Guacamole was less than a quarter mile from the parkway on Highway 70. Arroz con pollo sounded like the perfect dinner. I'm a big fan of Mexican food.

My family ate a lot of Mexican food when I was growing up. I grew up in Springdale, Arkansas a small town that boasted many quality hole-in-the-wall Mexican eateries. My paternal grandmother is from the Dominican Republic, which also had influence over our food preferences.

I ordered the chicken and rice plate and added onions and green peppers. It came smothered in white cheese sauce. Scott devoured his breakfast burrito. It was a late lunch and we were hungry. The restaurant had all kinds of salsas to try for free at their salsa bar from mild to super-hot and all different colors: red, green, orange, and dark, brownish red. We sampled them with an unlimited amount of chips.

After fueling up we kept on our course. About twelve miles after lunch we crossed the bridge spanning the French Broad River. It was our low point for today at 2,100 feet. Our destination, Mount Pisgah Campground, was near 5,000 feet. The campground was about fifteen miles from the river. We had a lot of elevation to gain.

This stretch of road was slow going. We stopped at a few overlooks but mostly kept going. I kept looking at my bike computer, trying not to let my miles per hour drop below ten. Even with starting much later than expected, we made it to the campground just when we wanted, close to supper.

Before finding a site, we ate at the swanky, yet woodsy restaurant at the Pisgah Inn. Without taking the time to change, we wore our bike shorts with pride, not caring what other people thought of our attire. Despite our appearance, we thought it fitting to treat ourselves to a good meal. I had Pisgah Pasta: a crème sauce dish with mushrooms, cherry tomato halves, fresh spinach, and grilled chicken. A sweet Pinot Nior complimented the meal.

I was freezing in the restaurant. I attributed it to the six or seven glasses of ice water. The waitress got tired of refilling our glasses and set a pitcher at our cramped table for two. The restaurant had huge windows overlooking the lower foothills to the East. The view was spectacular, but I concentrated more on the décor around the room. I mused that they were "richifying" the woods, making it more artsy and sophisticated to appeal to the upper class. I'd take the outdoors in its natural beauty any day. To think the restaurant was trying to emulate nature must mean there's some sort of innate wonder and beauty about it.

Our campground has a shower! It was dusk when I walked to the bathhouse after setting up my tent. The single stall was vacant. I plopped my clothes on the bench and turned on the water. If I could sleep standing up, I would have spent the night here. The pressure was great, and the warmth soothed my muscles. My whole body was able to relax. Not knowing if there were people waiting their turn, I reluctantly reached for the nozzle, dried off, and walked back to my tent in the pitch-black night.

# Forty-eight, Six-O-One

*July 26*

───────────～───────────

I thought I wasn't going to get any sleep last night. This campground wasn't overcrowded, but it was the busiest one we've been to. The young couple in the campsite next to ours started a movie on their laptop shortly after I laid down in my sleeping bag. I was furious inside my little tent. Why in the world would someone go into nature to camp, only to bring a laptop and movies? It seemed the very opposite of unplugging and "roughing it". I wished their battery would die or they would reconsider their plan to stay at the campsite.

Thankfully, I didn't remember anything after the opening trailers; I must have crashed when I put away my journal and pen. This morning both Scott and I woke up refreshed. We were hydrated, well-fed, I had a glorious shower last night, and we were camping in the high mountain forests of the Appalachians. What more could we ask for?

We decided to forgo breakfast at the restaurant to get an earlier start. Two Cliff Bars were all I had for my morning meal. I like the white chocolate macadamia nut, blueberry crisp, and oatmeal raisin walnut the best. I can't remember which ones I had today.

Soon after we got on our bikes, thick mist enveloped everything. Nearby, we could actually see the clouds whirling over the trees. They blew up from the valley on our left, which was East. We could hardly see the turns in the road fifty feet ahead and clicked on our front and rear lights. The purpose of our lights wasn't to aid our ability to see, but to help others see us. We've had such good luck with cars that we didn't want to ruin our trip out of unsafe neglect on our part. We weaved through the clouds until the sun rose high enough to burn them away. A precursor to the clouds dissipating, we've found, is rising temperature.

Later, during the day, I thought I was losing my breath quicker due to the higher elevation, but my mind may have just been playing tricks on me. When we reached the highest point on the parkway, I was a shocked we were already there. The ascent to Richland Balsam wasn't as daunting as I thought it was going to be. The road grade that scared me so much when we visited the Blue Ridge Music Center wasn't that bad. My legs must have gotten used to the climbing, because I felt our second day was much more grueling.

We set our bikes near the large sign that told us we were 6,053 feet above sea level. We asked a motorcyclist to snap a few pictures of us with our bikes. He graciously obliged. We took a few ourselves too, when no one was around, hanging off the sign and making silly faces. After a quick snack sitting on the rock wall contemplating the trip thus far, we went on our way.

No water at the Waterrock Knob Visitor Center surprised me. These seasonal sequesters have been a bit of a challenge for us, but one Scott and I have taken in stride. I wondered why they didn't have a spigot outside for motorists and bikers. This area boasted nearly a three-hundred- and sixty-degree view. The only parts we couldn't see far into the distance were to the North and South where the mountains piled up.

We rode past several picnicking families to a store that sold bottles of water for two dollars. I would rather find a stream. I can't stand when stores think they can rip people off just because they're the only ones around. But I didn't let their water monopoly sour my mood too long.

Scott drank a Coke as we talked with a man on a mountain bike who just beat his personal record to the knob by three minutes. We've seen several hardcore cyclists on this trip. I wouldn't consider myself even close to their level. We're just two normal guys with determination and a desire for adventure.

Scott read at the visitor center that the last eighteen miles were all downhill with the exception of two small inclines. We were excited to finally be near the end. Coasting down the spiral curves at the beginning were fun. We relaxed our legs, only using our arms to steer and brake. It was a different kind of work steering the curves and making sure we didn't go too fast. We were used to our muscles laboring on the lower half of our bodies most of the time. This time it was a little more mental. We had to be aware of how fast we were going and what was in front of us. We didn't really have to pedal as we reached the terminus.

Excitement soon gave way to boredom near the end though. It was almost too much downhill. Trees hung over the mountain side and obstructed our view. We had to keep our eyes pretty attuned to the road anyway. Tunnels broke up the dullness. There were a bunch of them.

We documented the end of our journey at the Mile Post 469 with a few pictures. There was no grand finale. The only thing that marked the end of the parkway was the humble mile post that looked just like all the others. We paused, each telling the other with surprise in our voices that we did it. We biked the whole thing.

Turning right on Highway 441, we rode to our pick-up point, the Oconaluftee Visitor Center for Smoky Mountain National Park. We set down our bikes for the last time. It was a mixture of relief and sadness. The ride was taxing on the body and mind. Most days we'd just eat, pedal, sleep, repeat. But the monotony of motion also allowed for deep thought, rich conversation with our Creator, and, of course, time to more fully appreciate the Appalachians. We had a goal each day we had to reach. It felt good to have a physical task to wake up to. I'm not sure what to look forward to tomorrow.

Audrey, a friend from back home in Southern Pines, got stuck behind slow moving cars on the five-hour drive. She called, apologizing that she'd be a littler later than expected. We didn't mind. It's not like we had anywhere we needed to be. We walked through the souvenir shop and history/ information area of the park. It couldn't have been a mile northwest from the parkway but, surprisingly, it had absolutely nothing about the parkway. Nothing at all. I couldn't believe it. I wonder if visitors to this area realize what's just down the road.

Audrey made it without too much delay. We loaded our bikes onto my rack I'd given her before we left. We made sure everything was strapped down well to her maroon car. Scott asked her to stop at Subway when reached Waynesville. He ran out of food at breakfast. I shared some peanuts and my remaining flour tortillas when we stopped at the highest point on the parkway, but we had done a lot of riding between then and now. I'd eaten two more Cliff Bars before reaching the visitor center, glad I'd purchased them in Spruce Pine, but I still wasn't full. We packed just enough food to get it through seven days.

Both of us ordered foot-long subs before going to Audrey's friend, Linda's house near Waynesville. Audrey helped set up our lodging weeks in advance and had a key. We wouldn't have driven back to Cameron Boys Camp tonight anyway. Camping was great, but a couch or bed has its perks too. We weren't too proud to enjoy this luxury.

Once we arrived at Linda's place, we waited for her to end her shift at the hospital. Both of us took showers. Mine was refreshing. I stayed in there as long as I could get away with without Scott or Audrey making fun of me. The couch was comfortable, and I slunk down in my clean, normal clothes I left with Audrey to bring. Everyone was totally content with doing nothing for a while. When Linda walked through the door, Scott and I introduced ourselves and thanked her for letting us stay. She'd never met us before. We were thankful Audrey had this connection.

Scott and I took a short walk around the neighborhood while the other two caught up and got ready. Once everyone had gotten ready to go out for the night, Linda drove us forty-five minutes Northeast to Asheville. It felt kind of crazy that we were there on bikes not too long ago.

We parked downtown and walked around Bele Chere, one of the largest outdoor street festivals in North Carolina. The festival boasted good music and art. Performers with guitars in hand were everywhere, not just on the multiple stages that were set up. Some were peddling for money, others just wanted to entertain an audience. Artists and creators came out of the woodwork to peddle their crafts. Woodcrafts, paintings, and various beadworks were all on display.

We made our way to a local pizzeria. Scott and I split a medium Mom's Garden Pizza, and I also ordered a quesadilla. We retold some of the adventures we experienced on the ride. The beautiful scenery was easily relatable and so were stories of people who helped us along the way like Jim and Susan, and Bill from Roanoke Mountain Campground, the people who gave us water, and those we interacted with at visitor centers.

What wasn't so easily grasped by Audrey and Linda was the hunger and fatigue we experienced; the brutal climbs, miles of nothing, hoping for water or a campsite at the end of the day, or the hard-earned joy and rest when we reached a peak. Those things we retold, but they didn't hold the weight to them like they did to Scott and me. Our shared experiences during the trip forged a greater understanding of each other.

A little over halfway into our conversation, we noticed an influx of people into the pizza parlor. It was a sign the bands had quit for the night. I didn't realize it was already past 10:00 p.m. It was time to finish the crust on my plate and walk back to the car. Luckily, we have all day tomorrow to explore the little shops and music venues at Bele Chere.

On forty-five-minute ride home, I had to force my eyelids open. Soon after getting to Linda's house, we wasted no time blowing up the inflatable mattress. I took the mattress this time. Scott took the couch.

We told a few more stories before saying goodnight. There would be no delay in going to sleep as soon as the light went out.

As Scott and I talked in the dark living room, both of us were in shock that we didn't have to ride tomorrow. The Blue Ridge Parkway adventure is over. I can't believe it. Four-hundred and sixty-nine miles still sounds like an unattainable goal, but we did it. I'm blessed to have the physical ability to take this ride. It was nearly a flawless ride. No crashes. No flat tires. No real gear malfunctions except for my panniers and bike chain. The weather was perfect. Nothing prevented us from riding every day.

I'm grateful for Chris and others, who encouraged me, and John who lent me the bike and urged me to go. And I'm thankful to have taken this ride with Scott. It was him who was most serious about it first. I wouldn't have tackled this adventure alone.

Southbound climb
48,601 feet

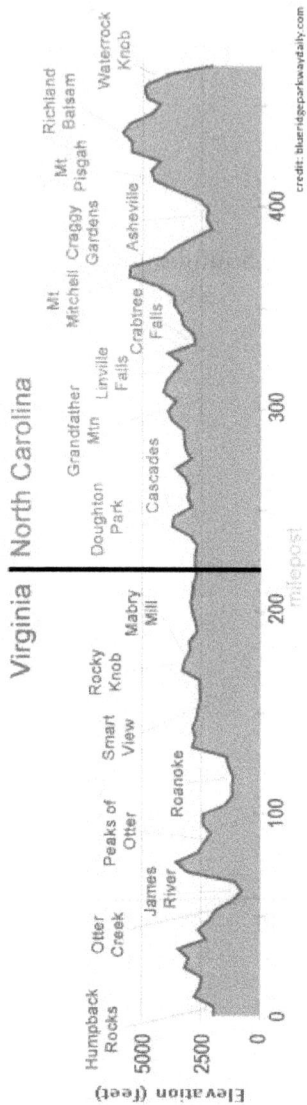

Virginia | North Carolina

Elevation (feet)

Humpback Rocks — Otter Creek — James River — Peaks of Otter — Roanoke — Smart View — Rocky Knob — Mabry Mill — Doughton Park — Cascades — Grandfather Mtn — Linville Falls — Crabtree Falls — Asheville — Mt Mitchell — Craggy Gardens — Mt Pisgah — Richland Balsam — Waterrock Knob

milepost

credit: blueridgeparkwaydaily.com

68

| Date | Day | Beginning Mile Post | Start | Stop | Ending Mile Post | Miles |
|---|---|---|---|---|---|---|
| July 20, 2013 | 1 | 0 | Rockfish Gap | Otter Creek Campsite | 60.9 | 60.9 |
| July 21, 2013 | 2 | 60.9 | Otter Creek Campsite | Roanoke Mountain Campground | 120.4 | 59.5 |
| July 22, 2013 | 3 | 120.4 | Roanoke Mountain Campground | Doughton Park | 241.1 | 120.7 |
| July 23, 2013 | 4 | 241.1 | Doughton Park | Julian Price Campground | 297.1 | 56 |
| July 24, 2013 | 5 | 297.1 | Julian Price Campground | Mineral Museum | 331 | 33.9 |
| July 25, 2013 | 6 | 331 | Mineral Museum | Mount Pisgah Campground | 408.6 | 77.6 |
| July 26, 2013 | 7 | 408.6 | Mount Pisgah Campground | Great Smoky Mountains SP | 469.1 | 60.5 |

Also by the Author

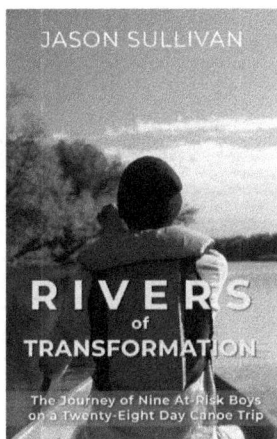

*Rivers of Transformation:*
*The Journey of Nine At-Risk Boys on a*
*Twenty-Eight Day Canoe Trip*